John Pamperin

Wisconsin jubilee

Proceedings of the celebration by the county and city of La Crosse on

Wisconsin

John Pamperin

Wisconsin jubilee
Proceedings of the celebration by the county and city of La Crosse on Wisconsin

ISBN/EAN: 9783337257453

Printed in Europe, USA, Canada, Australia, Japan

Cover: Foto ©Andreas Hilbeck / pixelio.de

More available books at **www.hansebooks.com**

WISCONSIN JUBILEE

PROCEEDINGS OF THE CELEBRATION

........BY THE.........

COUNTY AND CITY OF LA CROSSE

On Wisconsin having achieved fifty years

of statehood.

La Crosse County Historical Society organized May 28, 1898.

Grand Celebration held at La Crosse July 4, 1898.

REPUBLICAN AND LEADER PRINT,
LA CROSSE, WIS.

INTRODUCTORY

By R. Calvert, Secretary

On May 28, 1898, half a century having elapsed since the great State of Wisconsin cast off the habiliments of territorial youth and assumed the "toga virilis" of statehood, a general desire was manifested throughout its borders to make such a demonstration as would be a fitting testimony to its progress in the past, and an incentive to emulate it in the future.

The County of La Crosse, as it always does, quickly responded to the sentiment, and its County Board of Supervisors set the project in motion by an appropriation of $500 and the appointment of a Committee to carry it into effect.

The Committee consisted of W. C. Winter, N. R. Nelson, Frank Pooler, F. P. Coburn and Wm. Smith, and they at once invited the co-operation of all organizations throughout the County.

Several of these bodies responded, and a joint meeting was held at which were represented the Board of County Supervisors, the La Crosse Board of Trade, the Old Settlers Association and the La Crosse County Horticultural Society.

The subject was discussed pleasantly but earnestly, and while a general desire was manifested to commemorate the day by some ceremonial on the exact date, it was as generally believed that a larger attendance could be secured and more enthusiasm aroused on Independence day which was so near at hand.

After due discussion it was unanimously resolved to celebrate the 28th day of May by a public gathering and the organization of a Historical Association for the County, but that a popular demonstration upon a large scale should also be made on July 4th.

The following Executive Committee was elected to carry these ideas into effect:

John Pamperin.....................................La Crosse·
Hon. T. A. Dyson.................................La Crosse.
J. C. Burns......................................La Crosse.
N. R. Nelson.....................................La Crosse.
S. H. Russell....................................La Crosse.
R. Calvert.......................................La Crosse.
C. L. Lien.......................................La Crosse.
W. C. Winter.....................................La Crosse.
Paul W. Mahoney..................................La Crosse.
Frank Pooler.....................................Onalaska.
F. P. Coburn.....................................West Salem.
Edward Roessler..................................Siegel.
L. Cox...Mindora.
Wm. Smith..Bangor.
The joint Committee then adjourned "sine die."

On April 18, the Executive Committee met and organized by the election of

John Pamperin as Chairman,

R. Calvert as Secretary,

J. M. Holley as Treasurer,

and then proceeced to consider the requirements of the occasion.

A list of possible Committees was suggested and the Chairman authorized to report the same at an early date.

On April 25, the Committee again met, and the Chairman presented the following list of Committees which was unanimously approved:

Finance: J. C. Burns, R. A. Scott, Adam Kroner, J. C. Michel, J. P. Salzer, J. A. Elliott, Frank Bartl, J. O. Storey, H. J. Hirshheimer, J. L. Pettingill, P. W. Mahoney, S. H. Russell.

Speakers: James McCord, G. M. Woodward, A E. Bleekman.

Decorations and Floats: O. J. Oyen, G. M. Heath, L. W. Foster, H. Schick, C. F. Klein.

Grounds: Hon. T. A. Dyson, C. L. Lien, Geo. Zeisler, Jr., O. J. Sorrenson, Peter Nelson.

Fireworks: E. T. Mueller, F. S. Walker, Will Ott.

Music: W. A. Wiggenhorn, J. D. Hogan, William Goodrich.

Printing: W. C. Winter, N. R. Nelson, W. L. Kaeppler.

Transportation: W. L. Kaeppler, J. C. Burns, H. J. Hirshheimer.

River Regatta: F. A. Copeland.

Historical Society: Ellis B. Usher, chairman and the following members:

City of La Crosse, Dr. W. A. Anderson, G. R. Montague. W. L. Osborne, J. M. Levy, Mons Anderson, Chas. Michel, L. C. Colman, E. Wiggenhorn, Geo. Brice, Harvey Hubbard, J. S. Medary, W. Tarbox, H. A. Winston, C. N. McCain.

Barre...........Louis C. Sanders.

Bangor..........Wm. Smith, Dr. A. B. Newton, John Bradley, C. W. McKenzie, E. R. Roberts, John Wheldon.

Burns...........John N. Jones, L. R. Brown.

Campbell........John Dawson, C. H. Hawkins, John Johnson.

Farmington......L. B. Cox, Geo. B. Barber, John B. Hewitt, F. S. Brown, James H. Hodge, B. F. McClintock, Wm. F. Storandt, G. W. Mansergh.

Greenfield.......Herman Roessler, And. Boschert, H. Freehoff.

Holland.........Thos. Johnson, R. La Fleur.

West Salem......L. Lottridge, O. S. Sisson, A. McEldowney, Jesse Johnson, A. J. Philips, Jay Pettingill, Philip McConnell, Wm. Vanzandt, Daniel Shane, F. B. Smith, Davis Lewis, David Mc Clintock, J. W. Ramsey, John Coburn, F. P. Coburn, Phil. Quiggle.

Onalaska........Frank Pooler, M. M. Buttles, Chas. Farrand, Thos. Livingston, H. T. Wilhelm, C. G. Hall, Wallace W. Smith.

Shelby..........Chas. Linse, Peter Kienholz, E. Markie.

Washington......David Stromstad, John Strupp.

Later the untimely death of the Hon. T. A. Dyson created a vacancy which was filled by the appointment of Joseph Boschert on the Executive Committee and as Chairman of the Committee on Grounds.

These Committes at once assumed their several duties and reports of their labors will be found in their proper places, but it may be here stated that no set of Committees ever performed more laboriously and faithfully their several duties, nor achieved such perfect success, and at no period in the history of La Crosse County was there manifested such a spirit of enthusiasm, of hearty co-operation, and liberal response to all requirements.

The Executive Committee remained in almost continuous session and at their meetings, the following appointments were made:

President of the day........................Hon. J. W. Losey.

Vice Presidents for the towns.

Barre.....................................Geo. Sprain,
Bangor....................................W. A. Smith,
Burns.....................................John N. Jones.
Campbell..................................C. H. Hawkins,
Farmington................................Frank Storandt,
Greenfield...............................Herman Roessler,
Holland...................................A. H. Bratberg,
Hamilton..................................F. P. Coburn,
Onalaska..................................V. S. Keppel,
Shelby....................................Geo. A. Hosmer,
Washington................................Wenzel Korn,
West Salem................................Jay Pettingill,
City of Onalaska..........................Frank Pooler.

Vice Presidents, La Crosse City.

1st and 11th Wards........................A. Hirshheimer,
2nd and 12th Wards........................Mons Anderson,
3rd and 13th Wards........................J. M. Levy,

4th and 14th Wards........................David Austin,
5th and 15th Wards........................Wm. Gohres,
6th and 16th Wards........................C. L. Colman,
7th and 17th Wards........................C. Kurtenacker,
8th and 18th Wards........................John Gund, Sr.,
9th and 19th Wards........................Geo. H. Kingsley,
10th and 20 Wards........................Wm. H. Gordon.

Col. N. R. Nelson was appointed Chief Marshal with power to select his own aids and deputies.

The result of the combined labors of the Staff and Committees was the grandest demonstration ever attempted in the City of La Crosse, one which was in all respects a perfect success, a fitting tribute to the occasion which called it forth, an evidence of the prosperity and resources of the county and a convincing proof of the loyality and patriotism of its citizens.

Secretary.

CONTINUATION

BY JOHN PAMPERIN, CHAIRMAN OF THE

EXECUTIVE COMMITTEE.

The foregoing introduction suggests in a general way the scope of the task entrusted to the Executive Committee, but none but those who witnessed or participated in the proceedings can form an idea of the magnitude of the undertaking as it grew upon our hands, each Committee making valuable suggestions, which were all carefully considered, until the various ideas were moulded into a harmonious whole.

In laying the details before the subscribers the difficulty consists in knowing where to begin so as to make the narrative lucid and connected, and perhaps the best way will be to let each Committee tell its own story and then sum up the whole.

In all undertakings of this nature the first and most serious consideration is "ways and means" and in considering that question the Executive Committee felt very slight apprehension the County Board had laid a nest egg of liberal dimensions and the Committee relied upon the often tried and as often proved liberality of the Citizens of La Crosse to do the rest. That they were justified in their belief will be seen by the reports which ollow:

COMMITTEE ON A HISTORICAL SOCIETY.

The committee appointed in connection with this celebration, for the purpose of organizing a permanent County Historical Society as a memorial of the observance by the County of La Crosse of the golden anniversary of the State, beg leave to report as follows:

In order that all portions of the county should be represented, the committee was necessarily a large one, and a list of their names will be found in the roll of committees recorded by the Secretary in his introduction.

In response to the call of the Chairman, this committee met in the supervisors' room, in the Court House, in this city, at 2:00 o'clock p. m., on the second day of May. The following gentlemen were in attendance.

West Salem—Leonard Lottridge, Andrew McEldowney, O. S. Sisson, J. J. Johnson.

Campbell—John Dawson, C. H. Hawkins.

Onalaska—C. W. Farrand, Wallace Smith.

Shelby—Emanuel Markle.

Greenfield—H. Freehoff.

At this meeting Ellis B. Usher presided, and Lucius C. Colman acted as Secretary.

A committee was appointed, consisting of Leonard Lottridge, C. W. Farrand and L. C. Colman, who reported a plan of organization conformable to the statutes and to the rules laid down by the State Historical Society of Wisconsin for the organization of county societies auxiliary thereto, and their report was adopted.

The following named persons were selected by the meeting as officers, whose names should be used as incorporators, and who, under the law, would hold office until the annual election in November:

PRESIDENT—Ellis B. Usher.

VICE PRESIDENT—A. McEldowney.

SECRETARY—W. W. Jones.

TREASURER—M. M. Buttles.

ADVISORY COMMITTEE—G. R. Montague, John Dawson, L. B. Cox.

The committee was then continued with instructions to complete the legal organization and report at the meeting of the Old Settlers' Association, to be held at West Salem on May 28th.

On that date the committee reported that the legal organization had been duly effected, and that under the bylaws the monthly
meetings would be held on the first Tuesday in each month, except-
ing the months of June, July, August and September.

The annual dues were fixed at one dollar, and membership restricted to residents of La Crosse County. .

This statement comprehends all that is to be said of the purpose and accomplishments of this committee, up to date, but it is
believed that its work will result in much permanent value to this
county. The men and women, who are themselves its history, are
fast passing away, and it is of great importance that the record of
their lives should be preserved for the accurate information of
future historians. It is important that the autobiographies, biog-
raphies, portraits, personal mementoes, and all written doc ments
of these pioneers be preserved. Now is the time for this work to
begin, and the officers of the new society desire the co-operation of
every citizen of this county, to the end that a valuable collection
of such material may be gathered together.

Very respectfully submitted,

ELLIS B. USHER,

Chairman of the Committee for the Organization of a

County Historical Society.

COMMITTEE ON FINANCE.

Your Committee on Finance, having received the estimates of the requirements of the various other committees, although the total amount seemed large, were not discouraged, for they believed that the hearts of the people were as large as the sum needed, and at once commenced an active canvas. They foresaw that a great area of ground had to be gone over, and many people seen, in order to be successful, but they had the valuable assistance of the Chairman of the Executive Committee and others outside of their own body.

The following is a statement of the total amount collected and the names of the subscribers:

Appropriation from the Board of County Supervisors....	$ 500 00
Subscriptions from citizens, as per list..................	2,587 50
Sale of tickets for seats at fireworks....................	352 80
Received from Driving Association for use of band.......	25 00
	$3,465 30

LIST OF SUBSCRIBERS.

Estate of G C Hixon, by F P Hixon........	$100 00	L W Foster...........	10 00
J J Hogan.............	100 00	Richardson & Frye....	10 00
The National Bank of La Crosse..........	100 00	L Coren	10 00
John Gund Brewing Co	100 00	Harry Miller..........	10 00
G Heileman Brewing Co	100 00	Wiele & Schildman....	10 00
C & J Michel Brew. Co	100 00	Paul Malin............	10 00
C L Colman...........	100 00	Forschler & Hosly.....	5 00
P & W Cigar Co.......	50 00	H. Heil & Sons........	5 00
Hon Levi Withee......	50 00	John Hundt...........	5 00
Losey & Woodward ...	50 00	J Neukomm...........	5 00
John Paul Lumber Co..	50 00	F J Toland............	5 00
La Crosse City Ry Co..	50 00	Wilhelm-Nelson Carpet Co..................	5 00
Batavian Bank........	50 00	A Wehausen..........	5 00
Sawyer & Austin	50 00	W J Hickisch.........	5 00
George Zeisler & Sons..	35 00	Holmes & Bigelow.....	5 00
La Crosse Plow Co.....	25 00	John Wacker.........	5 00
John C Burns	25 00	C S Van Auken........	5 00
		James G Miller.........	5 00

J B Funke Co	25 00
Hon James McCord	25 00
The La Crosse Groc. Co	25 00
J S Medary Saddlery Co	25 00
M Kratchwill	25 00
A Platz	25 00
C B Dickson	25 00
Elliott-Loeffler Co	25 00
State Bank of La Crosse	25 00
Security Savings Bank of La Crosse	25 00
La Crosse Cracker and Candy Co	25 00
E R Barron Co	25 00
Wendell A Anderson	20 00
W W Cargill	25 00
German American Bank	25 00
N H and W W Withee	25 00
J A Salzer Seed Co	25 00
F S Walker	25 00
S Y Hyde	25 00
F A Copeland	25 00
F Bartl	25 00
B E Edwards	20 00
J C Easton	20 00
J L Pettingill	20 00
Cameron House	20 00
William Doerflinger	15 00
Segelke Kohlhaus Mfg. Co	15 00
M Funk Boiler Works	10 00
Adam Kroner	10 00
Smith Mfg. Co	10 00
Stavrum & Hulberg	10 00
Voigt & Ritter	10 00
B Ott & Sons	10 00
The La Crosse Plumbing Supply Co	10 00
T H Spence Drug Co	10 00
W A Strauss	5 00
John Rackelman	5 00
E C Josten	5 00
Stuve & Thompson	5 00
Charles H Marquardt	5 00
M & C Newberg	5 00
John Timp	5 00
W M Bronson	5 00
Robinson & Lyons	5 00
M F Hayes	5 00
B L Strouse & Co	5 00
J A Girk	2 00
A B Moll	5 00
Charles B Gesell	5 00
W T Irvine	5 00
Fruit & Gordon	5 00
Linker Bros	5 00
R C Kuhn Sash & Door Co	5 00
Weston & Simon	5 00
J B Hettinger	5 00
William Neibuhr	5 00
John G Malin	5 00
McConnell & Schweizer	5 00
Ed Richardson	5 00
Joseph Gutman	5 00
Bloom & Berger	5 00
T D Servis	5 00
W A Roosevelt Co	5 00
H A Loeffler & Co	5 00
Batchelder & Son	5 00
Miller & Wolfe	5 00
Hebberd & Co	5 00
A V Fetter	5 00
J A Erhart & Son	5 00
La Crosse Book & Stationery Co	5 00
Hon John Brindley	5 00
R Elliott	5 00

H Noll	10 00	William Franz	5 00
Langdon & Boyd	10 00	C A Sterling	5 00
Odin J Oyen	10 00	George P Rog..e	5 00
Tillman Brothers	10 00	A Bellerue	5 00
V Tausche Hdw. Co	10 00	W E Hadley	5 00
F A Shaldach	10 00	C Abnit	5 00
Jule Freas	10 00	Bergonst Grocery Co	5 00
J I Lamb	10 00	Jehlen Bros	5 00
M Guenther	10 00	F Solomon	5 00
La Crosse Boot & Shoe		Grand Union Tea Co	5 00
Mfg Co	10 00	A M Watson	5 00
Peter Newberg	10 00	Nic Kaiser	5 00
A Gilbertson	10 00	M B Stathem	5 00
Davis, Sorensen & Co.	10 00	Frank G Roth	5 00
W J Boycott	10 00	H H Byrne	5 00
H T Waters	10 00	Dr Gatterdam	5 00
Seielstad & Haugen	10 00	John James & Co	5 00
Bleekman, Bloomingd'le		I G Loomis	5 00
& Bergh	10 00	R A Scott	5 00
John Dengler	10 00	William Lohmiller	2 50
Palmer & Son, Livery	5 00	M E Mosher	10 00
Drs Powell & Powell	10 00	L Frey	20 00
M Tourtellotte	10 00	Hon G H Ray	10 00
A Lautz	5 00	Fred Kroner Co	10 00
L Kleeber	5 00	S Gantert	5 00
M Wannebo	5 00	Hotel La Crosse	5 00
J M Vrchota	5 00	C Beysthlag	5 00
O H Tyler	5 00	J Ebner	5 00
N Haerter	5 00	J Collins	5 00
Higbee & Bunge	5 00	Mons Anderson	10 00
N C Bacheller	5 00	J A Trane	5 00
Yeo & Clark	5 00	J S O'Connor	3 00
		Board of Supervisors	500 00

$3,087 00

All these amounts were promptly paid and turned over to the Treasurer, and his statement and the reports of the other subcommittees will show how the money was expended.

I should be wanting in courtesy if I failed to acknowledge the cheerful manner in which every member threw himself into the work, and to emphasize the fact that the people of La Crosse, both in county and city, can always be relied upon for a generous response to the call of a proper occasion.

Respectfully submitted,

JOHN C. BURNS,
Chairman Finance Committee.

COMMITTEE ON DECORATIONS AND FLOATS.

The Committee on Decorations beg leave to report that the work was systematised, divided and carried out as follows:

The arch and street decorations were placed in charge of Mr. Hugo Schick, and in this he had the valuable assistance of all the Committee; Mr. G. M. Heath solicited the co-operation of the Merchants and Manufacturers in the display of floats, and aroused interest in the floral carriage display, in which he was ably assisted by Mrs. W. W. Cargill who took charge of that feature of the event.

Mr. C. F. Klein enlisted the secret and benevolent societies and similar bodies with much success.

Mr. L. W. Foster superintended the gathering and organizing of the children for the red, white and blue floats of the Executive Committee a task in which he was ably assisted by Miss Bertha Riek. Mrs. L. H. Peck and Mrs. F. H Fowler.

The Committee believe that the result of their labors fully repaid the efforts and time expended on the work: they feel that with the limited time allowed, only the hearty co operation of all concerned enabled them to do so much and keep the expense within the amount appropriated to their department.

ODIN J. OYEN,
Chairman.

COMMITTEE ON GROUNDS AND STANDS.

Your Committee on Grounds and Stands submit their report as follows:

They erected a large platform on the east side of the Court House with 2,000 feet of seating capacity, and a band stand adjoining; they provided a reviewing stand with comfortable seats for the ex-Mayors at the Main entrance to the City Building on State Street; they arranged 7,500 feet of seats on the new park at the public landing for parties to enjoy the fireworks, and band stands at the northeast and northwest corners of the enclosure. They distributed 2,050 complimentary tickets to subscribers and members of the various committees and sold to others a number sufficient to realize $352 80. In order to do this they had to some what exceed their appropriation but were thereby enabled to realize for the general fund a net surplus of $177.38.

The Committee are indebted to the Board of Public Works for valuable assistance in laying off and preparing the grounds, and to the Chief of Police for his hearty and successful co-operation in maintaining order during the evening.

Respectfully submitted,

JOSEPH BOSCHERT,
ORI J. SORENSEN,
GEO. ZEISLER, Jr.,
C. L. LIEN,
PETER NELSON,
Committee.

COMMITTEE ON MUSIC.

The Committee on Music herewith submit a report of the arrangements made by them towards the success of this great celebration. On being appointed they directed their efforts to secure as much and as good music as possible and they have a reason to believe that those efforts were successful.

The length of the parade required a judicious distribution of the music, but having procured six bands and a drum corps, a good effect was attained. Arrangements were also made for three of these bands to play at several points during the afternoon and two of them played at the public landing during the evening until after the fireworks. For the use of one of the bands during the afternoon at the driving park the Committee received $25.00 and were thus enabled to return $28.55 of their appropriation to the general fund.

Respectfully submitted,

WM. A. WIGGENHORN,
JOHN D. HOGAN,
W. F. GOODRICH,
Committee.

COMMITTEE ON PRINTING.

The Committee on Printing, in submitting their financial report, beg leave to make the following statement of the work done by them.

Circular letters, advertising cards and posters were distributed throughout the territory within a radius of one hundred miles of La Crosse. In addition to this, advertisements were put in the four daily papers published in the city. In connection with this work, we desire to particulary mention the assistance rendered us by the wholesale houses of the city and their traveling salesman, in distributing advertising cards and posters in territory not reached by the railroads. We also wish to mention the work done by the newspapers of the county, in booming the celebration.

That the work of your committee was not in vain, can be judged by the ten thousand visitors that were attracted to the city to see the celebration.

W. C. WINTER,
Chairman.

COMMITTEE ON TRANSPORTATION.

To the Committee on Transportation was assigned the duty of arranging accommodation for bringing the people of our own and adjacent states to attend our great celebration.

The committee realized that to insure a large attendance ample facilities must be arranged, both for arrival and departure, and their efforts were directed in that direction.

The Chairman, under instructions, communicated with the agents of the various railroad lines entering the city, and with the masters of several steamboats available for passenger service. The preliminary work was rather discouraging, as the great demand for rolling stock at all points on that day precluded extra trains being fur ished to this point, but after much correspondence and great personal exertions, the difficulties were fairly met and reasonable means of transportation provided for.

All trains on all the lines were well patronized, and your committee believe that if the railroad companies had made a rate of one fare for the round trip they would have carried double the number.

Capt. Kratka brought from Lansing and other points on the steamer Pauline over 300.

Capt. Wilcox, on the Lion, brought 400 from Fountain City; Capt. Buisson, with the C. W. Cowles, brought 1,000, and on the Lotus Capt. Case brought 500 from Winona and intermediate points.

The Street Railway brought 1,000 people from Onalaska and the crowds who came by teams from all points of the compass poured in a continuous stream from dawn until nearly noon.

Your committee submit the following estimate of visitors who neighbored with us on that day:

By all the railroads..... 3,570
By all boats................................ 2,400
From country, via Onalaska............... 1,000
From country, by team.................... 1,500

The latter is a very conservative estimate, and the committee feel assured that the total figures are under, rather than over, the mark. The total attendance from abroad was thus 8,470.

Your committee desire to thank the agents of the various transportation companies for their courtesy and the cheerful cooperation which they rendered, and also to express their obligations to the Executive Committee of the Manufacturers and Jobbers' Union for their timely and effectual assistance.

Respectfully submitted,

W. L. KAEPPLER,
JOHN C. BURNS,
H. J. HIRSHHEIMER,
Committee on Transportation.

REPORT OF COMMITTEE ON SPEAKERS.

Your Commitce on Speakers found some difficulty in procuring a speaker worthy of the occasion, eloquence on that day being in great demand, but they are happy in being able to report that they succeeded beyond their most sanguine expectations.

It will be conceded by all who heard the Hon. Eugene Elliott that his speech on that occasion was an effort such as we are rarely privileged to hear, whether viewed trom an oratorical standpoint or as an exposition of all that was desirable to be avoided or emulated in the place which, as a people, we have taken among the nations of the earth.

Its effect was heightened by the reccipt on the platform of the news of the destruction of the Spanish fleet of Admiral Cervera, of which the President of the day availed himself to punctuate his remarks.

Respectfully submitted,
JAMES McCORD,
G. M. WOODWARD,
A. E. BLEEKMAN,
Committee.

REPORT OF TREASURER.

RECEIPTS.

From	County Board	$500 00	
"	City subscriptions	2,587 50	
"	Seats on public landing	352 80	
"	Hire of band at Driving Park	25 00	$3,465 30

DISBURSEMENTS.

For	Street and other decorations	$900 00	
"	Stands, platforms, etc	175 42	
"	Bands, music, etc	491 45	
"	Speakers' committee	113 65	
"	Fireworks	799 25	
"	Advertising and printing	194 49	
"	Carriages for speakers, etc	7 00	
"	Badges, and printing same	18 50	
"	Medals for same	13 00	
"	Silk flag for Marshal	2 00	
"	Expenses of Marshal's office	2 70	
"	Expenses of Secretary, postage, etc	6 60	2,724 06

Surplus $741 24

Less 25 per cent. of $2,587.50 returned to
subscribers. Circulars, revenue stamps
and postage distributing same......... 654 93

Balance on hand to be used in publication
and distribution of this pamphlet...... 86 31

JOHN M. HOLLEY,
Treasurer.

PROCEEDINGS OF THE MORNING.

REPORT OF CHIEF MARSHAL.

I herewith submit the following report comprising the features, incident to the duties assigned to me in connection with the Semi-Centennial Celebration on July 4th, 1898.

The day was all that could be desired, clear and cool, an ideal day for the occasion and the individuals and bodies participating were requested to report promptly at 10 A. M., to the assistant Marshals respectively commanding the divisions to which they were assigned. I am pleased in being able to say that all responded, so that the procession was fully organized and moved promptly at 10:30 as arranged.

It was composed of eight divisions, each commanded by an assistant Marshal and moved in the following order, led by

Platoon of Police in charge of Capt. Parks.
Col. N R Nelson, Chief Marshal
and his personal staff.
Norris Batchellor, Chief of Staff.

C. S. Van Auken	Archie Morse
John Michel, Jr.	J. O. Storey
J W. Losey Jr.	J. L. Hougan
Dr. Frank Weston	Adelbert Miller
J. P. Salzer	H. A. Lavake

FIRST DIVISION.

Assistant Marshal, Martin Bergh.

Langstadt's Band.
Wilson Colwell Post, G. A. R.
John Flynn Post, G. A. R
City of La Crosse Letter Carriers.

CARRIAGES CONTAINING

J. W. Losey, President of the Day.
Hon. Eugene Elliott. Speaker.
Hon. James McCord, Mayor.
John Pamperin, Chairman Executive Committee.
The Vice Presidents of the County.

The Vice Presidents of the City.
County Board of Supervisors.
County Officials.
Common Council of the City.
City Officials.
Board of Education.
Executive Committee.

SECOND DIVISION.

Assistant Marshal, Clarence B. Dickson.
Professor Hamre's Band of Preston.
United Commercial Travelers—Red.
Benevolent and Protective Order of Elks
and float—White.
Catholic Order of Foresters—Blue.
Norden Society.
Germania Float and Guard.
Liederkranz, Normanna, Frohsinn, Orpheus,
Concordia and Fidelia Singing Societies.
Fidelia Float and Guard.

THIRD DIVISION.

Assistant Marshal, John E. Langdon.
Zouave Drum Corps.
Third Ward Aid Society and Float.
La Crosse Valley Lodge, I. O. O. F.
Gateway City Lodge, I. O. O. F.
Normanna Lodge, I. O. O. F.
Modern Woodmen Camp.
C. S. P. S. Society.
Concordia Society.
Young Men's Christian Association, 50 Boys,
Uniformed.

FOURTH DIVISION.

Assistant Marshal, J. G. Miller.
Ladies' Onalaska Band.
Three floats of the Executive Committee in red, white and blue,
representing part of a gunboat fleet.

24

DISPLAY OF FLORAL CARRIAGES.

Professor Toland's new English "brake." The decorations were red and white chrysanthemums and blue corn flowers. The occupants were Messrs. Lee Toland, Albert Scharpf, Harry Long, Bert Campbell and Neumeister.

Mayor James McCord; carriage decorated with blue corn flowers; dark bay team. Mrs. McCord, Miss Cora Bennett and Miss Miss Agnes McCord.

Hon. Levi Withee's trap; yellow and white chrysanthemums. Mr. Abner Withee and Miss Jennie Smith.

Mrs. G. C. Hixon; victoria, with light and dark heliotrope chrysanthemums; black horses. Mrs. Munson Burton and Miss Mary Crosby.

Mr. L. C. Colman; pink chrysanthemums. Mr. and Mrs. Colman, Misses Grace Wyckoff and Laura Osborne.

Mr. James Vincent; white chrysanthemums and green foliage, white trappings. Mrs. Vincent, Mrs. Bloomingdale, Miss McKillip and Miss Agnes Vincent.

Mr. Mills Tourtellotte; trap with red carnations and ivy leaves, grey team. Mr. and Mrs. Tourtellotte, Miss Eleanor McDonald and Miss Lillian Tourtellotte.

Mr. Geo. M. Heath; purple morning glories, black team. Mrs. Heath, the Misses Mildred Holley, Grace Burroughs and Grace Heath.

P. S. Davidson; pink chrysanthemums, grey horses, Mr. W. F. Davidson, Mrs. P. S Davidson, Mrs. Joseph Skinner and Miss Helen Burton.

Mr. and Mrs. W. W. Withee were in a trap decorated with yellow chrysanthemums, and drawn by black horses.

Mr. and Mrs. F. J. Tolard; spider phaeton, covered with white chrysanthemums, black horse.

Mr. F. A. Copeland's carriage, red chrysanthemums, Miss Marie Louise Copeland, Miss Irene Copeland and Miss Fanny Rodolf.

Mr. S. Y. Hyde's trap; yellow chrysanthemums. Mr. Robert Hyde, Miss Georgina McDonald, and Mr. and Mrs. Arthur J. Pitkin.

Dr. Main and Miss Irma Berger, phaeton with lavender chrysanthemums; whit horse with white trappings.

Mr. Stephen Gantert, bay team, carriage decorations, pink chrysanthemums. Mr. Gantert, Mrs Ross, Miss Gantert and Miss Sophia Gantert.

Mr. Albert Platz; purple and white chrysanthemums. Mrs. Platz, Miss Linda Berger, Miss Gretchen Salzer, Miss Caroline Lloyd and Mr. Albert Platz.

Mr. John Gund Jr., yellow and white chrsanthemums; Cleveland bay team. Mr. and Mrs Gund and Mrs. H. L. Colman.

Mr. Gysbert Van Steenwyk; blue corn flowers. Mrs. Mollie Austin, Miss Louise McDonald and Miss May Van Steenwyk.

Mr. F. P. Hixon, team of Cleveland bays; carriage decorations pink chrysanthemums. Mrs. Hixon and Miss Wagner of Chicago.

Mr. Charles Michel; white chrysanthemums. Miss Michel, Miss Freda Michel and Mrs. Luening.

Mr. W. W. Cargill; red roses and smilax. Miss Cargill and Miss Jessie McMillan.

Mr. W. R. Montague, trap; decorations of red, white and blue. Mr. and Mrs. Montague, Miss Helen Edwards and Miss Eva Bennett.

Mr. Eugene Derr's cart; white chrysanthemums. Master Lester Derr and the Misses Lilah and Edith Derr.

The Misses Marie Wheeler and Bessie Taylor; cart with white daisies.

Mr. Samuel Hyde, Mr. Robert Gordon, Miss Louisa Gund and Miss Ruth Heath; cart, red, white and blue.

FIFTH DIVISION.
Assistant Marshal, Nicholas Groff.

North La Crosse Band.
Catholic Societies, arranged by the Marshal commanding,
Division Uniform Ranks at the head.
St. Joseph Society.
St. Bonifacious Society.
St. Aloysius Society.
St. Mary's Catholic Knights.
Hibernians, North and South.

St. John's Society, North La Crosse.
Bohemian Society, North La Crosse.
Schaller's Drum Corps.
St. Georgius Knights.
St. Wenceslaus Society.
St. John's Society.
Polish Congregation.
Holy Cross Society.
National Aid Society.
Polish Guards.
Holy Trinity Congregation.
Holy Trinity Society.
Luxemburger Society.
St. Stanislaus Society.

SIXTH DIVISION.

Assistant Marshal, Dr. F. C. Suiter.

Greenfield Band.
Greenfield Exhibit and Troop of Rough Riders.
Bangor Exhibit.
Burns Exhibit.
Campbell Exhibit.
Farmington Exhibit.
Holland Exhibit.
Hamilton Exhibit.
Onalaska Exhibit.
Shelby Exhibit.
Washington Exhibit.
West Salem Exhibit.
City of Onalaska Exhibit.

This division was closed by the ward floats, many of which were well gotten up. The Eighth Ward went to the least trouble, and the "exhibit" caused as much talk as anybody's. It consisted of a road cart, a keg of beer and a sign, "The Bloody Eighth."

Besides this that ward had a float containing a number of pretty little girls in red, white and blue.

The Fourth Ward wagon contained an old log cabin and Indians.

The Seventh Ward had a large wagon representing the United States, to which was attached smaller wagons representing Cuba, the Philippines, Puerto Rico and Hawaii.

The Eleventh Ward had a float, and "Goosetown" was well represented by two large ganders in a cage.

The float of the Thirteenth Ward attracted much attention. It represented Columbia, surrounded by the thirteen original states, all represented by beautiful young ladies, receiving Wisconsin into the Union, and was both original and suggestive.

SEVENTH DIVISION.

Assistant Marshal, R. A. Scott.

This may be designated as the Industrial and Commercial Division, and was led by

The Bangor Band.

The C. H. Nichols Lumber Company, of Onalaska, came first with a load of their productions. Then a primitive ox team and prairie schooner, labeled "1848; poor roads and poor loads." Immediately following came a fine team of horses with a huge load of wheat in a strictly up-to-date wagon. This represented "1898; good roads and good loads."

The float representing the five breweries in the city was one of the most elaborate in the parade. Carl Urkwitz, of the Tivoli, seated on the throne, impersonated Gambrinus. A number of festive gnomes were around him. The float was drawn by ten horses.

The Fred Kroner Hardware Company had a large float drawn by six horses. It contained a fine display of their line of goods.

The Mons Anderson Company's float represented an old fortress.

J. J. Hogan displayed "Our Territory," showing La Crosse with its fine shipping facilities.

The Segelke-Kohlhaus Company was well represented.

The float of the Pamperin & Wiggenhorn Cigar Company represented the Cuban tobacco industry. It was driven by a man in Cuban costume. This display was one of the most beautiful and artistic features in the parade. Louis Tillman represented Ibykus, and at his feet were three pretty black haired girls, (the Misses

Birdsell) who represented Cuban girls. The company received many compliments on its novel display.

The La Crosse Grocery Company, Salzer Seed Company and the La Crosse Plow Company followed. Each had a float appropriate to their respective lines of business.

John C. Burns was out with three wagons, the first containing a display of fruits.

Voigt & Ritter displayed a fine wagon built by them for the C. & J. Michel Brewing Company.

The Funk Boiler Works exhibited a huge boiler, and another one with men at work.

O. J. Oyen, who deserves much credit for the decorations in the parade, had a handsome float, drawn by four horses. Louis Oyen was busily engaged in displaying wall paper.

M. B. Stathem displayed a huge rooster, representing his market.

The Listman Mill Company had an interesting display of Marvel flour. Small bags were given out as souvenirs.

The Champion binder had a float and thirty men in line.

The New Home Sewing Machine Company was represented by Volz, Bros. & Reuter.

The V. Tausche Hardware Company was out with a battleship.

Devine & Baker, tile sidewalk men, and the Reed and Rattan Works each had a creditable float.

The La Crosse Soap Company had a wagon with a pretty little home, representing "Sweet Home" Soap.

Frank G. Roth had a float built on two tandems. It represented his business and advertised the "Crescent" bicycle.

Adam Kroner showed a line of hardware.

John James & Co., the Pioneer Foundry, had an interesting display of a steam engine and well drilling machinery.

Other floats and displays were in the parade as follows:

George Will, groceries; Schnell Bros., brick; J. E. Willing, shoes; Doud & Sons, coopers; W. A. Roosevelt Company, plumbing supplies; Gateway City Marble Works; Modern Steam Laundry; La Crosse Plumbing Supply Company; H. A. Loeffler & Company, George Herken; The Franklin Iron Works; Bailey & Weis, Books and Wall Paper; The La Crosse Bakery; Warninger and Houthmaker. mineral and aerated waters; M. Hirshheimer, tents and awnings; J. H. Marden, tile work; The Gateway City Laundry; North Side Bottling Works; The Star Laundry; Will C. Free, Sewing Machines; The Reliance Boiler Works and many others.

EIGHTH DIVISION.

Assistant Marshal, Captain C. A. Hunt.
Entire Fire Department and Apparatus.

This was the last and one of the best features of the parade the fire department being out in full force, men and apparatus. Everything was neat and clean which is one of the features of the La Crosse fire department under Chief Hunt's management. The apparatus were all decorated with flowers and flags.

The procession was nearly three miles in length, and the distance covered over forty blocks; the line of march was from the Market Square to Pearl street, west to Front, north to Main, east to Sixth, south to Cass, east to Eleventh, north to State, west to Fourth, north to La Crosse, west to Third. south to Jay and east to Market Square, where the divisions were dismissed, the time occupied by the march having been one hour and forty-five minutes.

In closing this report I desire to express my appreciation and grateful thanks to the Assistant Marshals, Aids, Chief of Staff and Staff for the cordial support given me, and which made it possible o move so large a procession without a single hitch.

I also embrace the opportunity of expressing my thanks to all who had to co oper te in the work done, and to say that special credit is due to Mrs. W. W. Cargill and the ladies who assisted her in the preparation of the beautiful floral display in the Fourth Division, which was a dream of beauty we are seldom privileged to enjoy.

Respectfully submitted,
N. R. NELSON,
Chief Marshal.

EXERCISES OF THE AFTERNOON.

The arrangement for the afternoon was a mass meeting of the citizens on the Court House Square at 2:30 p. m., to hear an address appropriate to the great event which they had turned out to celebrate, and the proceedings were in charge of

J. W. LOSEY, PRESIDENT OF THE DAY.

Mr. Losey was most felicitous in his remarks introducing the speaker to the people of La Crosse county. Patriotic music filled up the intervals, but grandest of all was the rousing, logical and eloquent speech of the Hon. Eugene Elliott, who held the great mass of people in spellbound silence, relieved by occasional bursts of deafening applause.

At the appointed hour the square was completely filled by an immense assemblage, and the grandstand was occupied by the County Board of Supervisors, the Mayor and Common Council, the ex-Mayors of La Crosse and the various officers of the day.

The adjoining stand was appropriated to Langstadt's Military Band and a male chorus, composed of the members of all the musical organizations of the city.

The proceedings were opened with an impressive prayer by

THE RIGHT REV. JAMES SCHWEBACH,

followed by the reading of the Declaration of Independence by the

HON. B. F. BRYANT.

At its conclusion Mr. Losey advanced to the front of the platform, and taking the document just read as his text, narrated in glowing language the conditions and events incident to its adoption, its effect upon the history of the day, and the impetus which it gave to the cause of liberty throughout the world.

At this point the following telegram was put into his hands, which he immediately read to the assembled crowd:

OFF SANTIAGO, July 4.—The fleet under my command offers to the nation as a Fourth of July greeting the destruction of the whole of Admiral Cervera's fleet. The Spanish fleet attempted to escape at 1:30 Sunday morning and at two o'clock the last of the Spanish ships, the Christobal Colon, had run ashore sixty miles west of Santiago and hauled down her colors. The Infanta Marie Teresa, Oquendo and Viscaya were forced ashore, burned or blown up within twenty miles of Santiago. The Pluton and Furor were destroyed within four miles of port. Our loss was two wounded and one killed. The enemies loss is probably several hundred from gun fire, explosions and drowning. Took about 1,300 prisoners including Admiral Cervera. Our man killed was George Ellis, chief yeoman of the Brooklyn.

SAMPSON.

The reading of the message was hardly concluded when the crowd broke forth into enthusiastic and prolonged cheers and when Mr. Losey called for three cheers for Admiral Dewey and the American Navy, they were repeated again and again, while the band played "Columbia the Gem of the Ocean," with a spirit which seemed caught from the enthusiasm of the occasion.

Order being at length restored, Mr. Losey in an eloquent and impassioned speech traced the history of the State of Wisconsin, from its territorial times until the present day; followed up the development of the County and City of La Crosse and dwelt lovingly upon the memories of its pioneers, many of whom had passed to their rest, while some of them were honored participants in the present celebration.

32

He then introduced as the orator of the day, the
HON. EUGENE ELLIOTT,
of Milwaukee, who spoke as follows:

H .manity has been a long time growing old. In the life of man, fifty years are a memorable period, but, in the life of races, centuries are the only mile stones of progress. There are no records by which we can determine how many thousand years man was a savage nor how many thousand more he was a barbarian; even the history of semi-civi'ization begins in doubt. Compared with the ordinary span of human life, the world is old ; but there is no reason to believe that, with all its age in years humanity has, as yet, grown beyond its youth. The tendency of the babe is to smash things ; before he is old enough to be called a reasoning being his predominant trait is pugnacity. So, of the race. Ancient history and the greater part of modern history is written in blood. Take from it the monotonous story of its wars, eliminate its Alexanders, its Caesars and its Napoleons and little remains to repay the researches of the student.

THERE IS NO HISTORY OF THE PEOPLE.

It is true that Grecian art is the despair of modern times ; it is true that Egyptian science paved the way for later discoveries, that schools of philosophy flourished and that the luxury of Rome has never been excelled, but these constituted only a veneer upon social conditions that was incapable of hiding the rottenness beneath.

INTELLIGENCE OF THE MASSES THE BASIS OF CIVILIZATION.

The masses of the people did not share and probably could but poorly comprehend the privileges enjoyed by the few. If there was learning in Greece and civilization in Egypt, never the-less Greece was not learned nor was Egypt civilized ; th ir learning and civilization were hot house plants indicative merely of what humanity was capable with proper cultivation ; before learning and civilization could be other than transitory and evanescent it was necessary that a suitable soil should be prepared in which they could take strong root. So for thousands of years we note the rise and growth and the decline and fall of empires, and the establishment and decay of ephemeral republics. Humanity was fertilizing itself, creating soil from which was destined to spring the luxuriant vegetation of the nineteenth century.

THE GOOD FORTUNE OF AMERICA.

It was the good fortune of America, and particularly of Wisconsin and her younger sister states, that their part in the world drama should begin when the evolution of our race from savagery to civilization had opened up fields for human enterprise that the wildest dreams of the idealist had not ventured to forecast.

It is the good fortune of Wisconsin, that upon the conclusion of her first fifty years of statehood, her people can look back upon a progress that is unexampled in the history of the world.

From the busy marts of trade, from the crowded city streets, from town and hamlet and verdant field, from the pine forest and the mill, we come to do honor to this anniversary. Surrounding us, on every side, are evidences of prosperity and happiness that only ample wealth combined with the highest culture, refinement and intelligence could have provided, yet, when Wisconsin was admitted to the dignity of statehood, only the advance guard of the mighty host that has followed was established here. The wilderness reigned supreme ; the home of the savage beast, and yet more savage man. Nathan Myrick was here, and John M. Levy, and shortly after Timothy Burns, but altogether less than an hundred people called what we now know as the county of La Crosse, their home. Thus men, yet in their prime, have been privileged to see during the short space of fifty years the grand evolution from savagery to the highest civilization ; an evolution that required, in the old world, sixty centuries to complete. Such a marvelous transformation could only have been accomplished by extraordinary men under the inspiration of extraordinary conditions.

The most modest merit could not fail to appreciate this fact, nor will it seek to deny itself the pleasure of felici ation upon its success. It will rather add to than detract from that pleasure to reflect that the congratulations due to this occasion are shared by the entire commonwealth of Wisconsin; for the sagacity, the thrift, the enterprise and the tenacity that achieved success for Western Wisconsin, exemplify similar traits in all parts of our great state. We content ourselves, therefore, with but a glance at events of

34

merely local importance to consider, briefly, the wider field of State affairs.

THE HISTORY OF THE STATE IS THE HISTORY AS WELL OF LA CROSSE COUNTY AND OF WESTERN WISCONSIN.

In the executive Chamber, in the Senate of the United States, in every department of our State government, you have been represented; your aid has been sought and given, your counsel has been asked and heeded in the conduct of every important event.

THE KEY NOTE OF SUCCESS.

The greatness of the State of Wisconsin was assured from the adoption of the constitution. The key notes of that greatness was struck in the guaranty of the inherent rights of life, liberty and the pursuit of happiness, of liberty of speech, of the covenant that "The right of every man to worship Almighty God according to the dictates of his own conscience, shall never be infringed nor shall any man be compelled to attend, erect or support any place of worship or to maintain any ministry against his consent; nor shall any control of or interference with the rights of conscience be permitted or any preference be given by law to any religious establishment or modes of worship; nor shall any money be drawn from the treasury for the benefit of religious societies or religious or theological seminaries," and in the provision that "The legislature shall provide by law for the establishment of district schools which shall be as nearly uniform as practicable; and such schools shall be free and without charge for tuition to all children between the ages of four and twenty years; and no sectarian instruction shall be allowed therein."

These wise enactments that embody within the fundamental law of our State the principle of freedom of action, of religious toleration, and of universal education, crystallize the results of a struggle that has been going on for thousands of years. Only in the Nineteenth century, only in the United States of America was such an event possible.

THE SPECIAL PRIVILEGES OF AMERICA.

We regard our rights of thought and action and educational privileges as matter of course ignoring the fact that in the greater part of the world today no such rights and no such privileges exist. Herein is the distinction between the vigorous and permanent civilization of America and the ephemeral civilization of the past; herein centers our confidence in the future of the great republic whose existence depends, not upon the whim or favor of a limited class, but upon the intelligent patriotism of the masses each one of whom, as a voter, is an integral part of the government.

SUPERVISION OF CORPORATIONS.

The framers of our State Constitution were pioneers in the incorporation within our organic law of another provision, not found in the constitutions of many of the older states, but which experience has proven to be of vital importance. I refer to the section prohibiting the creation of corporations by special act and reserving to the legislature the power of amendment and repeal.

There should never be any clash between the people and the corporations that they have created; their true interests are identical; the welfare of each depends upon the prosperity of the other nor, I apprehend, can antagonism arise between them that is not born of trespass upon equitable principles. But the best way to prevent a wrong is to keep and use, when necessary, the power to redress it. The ounce of prevention afforded by our constitution in this regard, has already been worth many pounds of cure.

WOMAN'S RIGHTS.

The same broad minded statesmanship that so readily devised means for the protection of rights and the redress of wrongs, was prompt to recognize the fact that woman is, by nature and should be before the law, the equal of man. It was the highest tribute that could have been paid to the pioneer women of our state that Wisconsin should have been one of the first to strike off the shackles with which the common law, so unjustly, fettered them. It was a noble compliment nobly deserved by a sex that has crowned our Wisconsin homes with purity, refinement and loving self-sacrifice and made of them shrines before which the incense of all that is good and beautiful and true is kept forever burning.

LOYALTY OF WISCONSIN TO THE REPUBLIC.

Fellow citizens: Wisconsin took her place among the sisterhood of states professing sincere loyalty to the constitution and laws of the great Republic. During the fifty years that have elapsed, she has never wavered in fidelity to those professions nor flinched when her loyalty was put to the test. In the great war for the preservation of the Union, she armed and sent forth to battle more than ninety thousand of her sons and from her substance, to sustain the government, promptly and cheerfully answered every demand. The statement of General Sherman that "We estimated a Wisconsin regiment as equal to an ordinary brigade," was no idle compliment to the merits of the Wisconsin soldier boys, for Wisconsin had more than one brigade of iron.

That the same patriotic loyalty that rocked the cradle of our infant state continues to be cherished in our hearts with undiminished fervor, is attested by the presence of this vast assemblage gathered to do honor to the birthday of our state by worthily celebrating the one-hundred and twenty-second anniversary of Independence Day.

WISCONSIN'S HOMAGE TO INDEPENDENCE DAY.

For half a century Wisconsin has done annual homage to the sentiments inspired and symbolized by this day and now, upon its return and upon this, the fifty-first birthday of our State, we come to renew our pledge of fidelity to the flag for which our fathers fought, to the Republic for which our brothers died.

This annual convention has never been an unmeaning ceremony, nor has it ever been inspired by sinister or unworthy motives; but, upon this occasion, added solemnity is given to our meeting by the fact that each breeze that sweeps from the south, "brings to our ears the clash of resounding arms."

For the first time since Appomattox we are at war; in its prosecution our government is entitled to and will receive the loyal support of every patriotic citizen, notwithstanding the fact that the contest has been forced upon us by circumstances beyond our control and comes unwelcome, unbidden and unsought.

Thirty-three years of profound peace had not healed the bruises nor enabled us to forget the horrors of war. It is true that during that time the American people had suffered repeated spasms of bellicose passions and that jingo statesmanship continued to be cultivated as a cheap way of winning popular applause; it is true

that the great American game was the twisting of the British lion's
tail, and that the amusement most thoroughly enjoyed was hearing
the British lion roar ; but it is no less true that the intelligent
judgment of intelligent people was averse to war. The solemn service of memorial day constituted an annual reminder of what war
cost and the often repeated reminiscences of the survivors of the
Grand Army, were indisputable evidence of the misery that foll)w-
ed in its wake Moreover, in this year of our Lord, One Thousand
Eight Hundred Ninety Eight, America was beginning to take heart
in the hope that a period of financial depression almost unprece-
dented in its history, had finally come to a close, and that the storm
of disaster, before which the sturdiest fortunes bent and broke, had
at last spent its fury. To men, who for five years had been strug-
gling to save the wreck of their e tates, war came as an intrusive,
unwe'come spectre at the feast of returning prosperity. It meant
to them a postponment of those good times that they had been
congratulating themselves, were not only coming but had already
come. It meant the imposition of war taxes on the necessaries of
life, thereby adding from a third to a half upon the cost of living ;
it meant a return to stamp duties—the most onerous and conse-
quently most odious of all forms of taxation.

THE WAR NOT JUSTIFIED BY ESTABLISHED AMERICAN DOCTRINE.

The misgivings caused by such considerations were not soothed
by the reflection that interference between Spain and Cuba was not
justified by any established American policy. It has been urged
that such interference was warranted by the Monroe doctrine, but
that statement is it correct. The declaration of President Monroe
was to the effect that the United States would regard as an un-
friendly act any attempt to extend the monarchical system of
Europe over any part of the Western hemisphere, but it was not
intimated by that memorable document, nor has it ever since been
made a part of our political creed, that it was our duty to intervene in the domestic quarrels of European nations and their American Colonies. There was no thought of intervention in the wars
that preceded the establishment of the various South American republics, and even when France invaded Mexico and attempted to
erect there an empire upon the ruins of the Mexican Republic,

Secretary Seward officially instructed Mr. Motley, our minister to Austria, that : ''The United States have neither a right nor any disposition to intervene by force in the internal affairs of Mexico, whether to establish or maintain a republican or even a domestic government there, or to overthrow an imperial or foreign one, if Mexico shall choose to establish or accept it.''

The narrow limits to which this address is necessarily restricted, precludes the possibility of taking more than a glance at facts that can not be disputed, and which prove that interference in Cuban affairs cannot be sustained, upon the ground that it is in accordance with a doctrine to which the honor of the United States has been pledged. It is equally true that such interference is antagonistic to principles that Washington and his associates were strenous in impressing upon American policy.

When the question of our flag was under consideration, Benjamin Franklin proposed the device of a rattlesnake, coiled as if to spring with the legend ''Don't tread on me,'' as peculiarly characteristic of the function which the Republic was expected to fill among the nations. He urged that the rattlesnade never went out of its way to attack and never attacked except in selfdefense, and then only after ample warning, but was venomous in defending its own rights and when it struck it killed.

The proposition was, fortunately, not adopted, but it shows how tenacious the founders of our government were in embodying the theory of isolation among our national maxims. They foresaw that the time must come when under the pressure of conditions that would then be deemed obligatory or yielding to military enthusiasm, or inspired by hope of conquest. the United States would be tempted to take a hand in the game of international politics; they foresaw that unless that temptation was successfully resisted, large standing armies and navies such as weighed down the older nations, must result; that alliances offensive and defensive would necessariiy follow, and that our institution would be strained by wars, whose objective motives in no wise benefited a people who were enabled by geographical position to conduct their own affairs secure from foreign interference so long as they minded only their own business.

THE WISE STATESMANSHIP OF PRESIDENT McKINLEY.

The skillful diplomacy of President McKinley, his generous forbearance of word and action, the cool determination with which he resisted all attempt to force him into unwarranted or ill advised measures, do equal credit to his head and his heart, and prove that he was alive to the supreme importance of averting war, if war, without dishonor, could be avoided. But though the president and the people were sincerely opposed to war, the greatest human skill, the wisest statesmanship was powerless to prevent it, and today we are at war, not because we want to fight, but because it is our duty to fight, and fight we will to the bitter end, let the consequences be what they may. For this is God's war.

"THERE IS A DIVINITY THAT SHAPES OUR ENDS."

If, when I began the study of American history, I had been an atheist, long before I could have finished my task I would have been forced to the conclusion that "there is a divinity that shapes the end of" nations as well as "men rough hew them how we will." Note how conditions interlock, how events link into a chain leading up to a government, free in practice as well as in theory, of the people, for the people and by the people. Such a government must depend for its perpetuity upon the patriotic intelligence of the masses who, knowing their rights, are capable of defending them. Its foundations could not have been laid in Europe where there were no people, otherwise competent, who were sufficiently strong in number to resist the attack that monarchical jealousies would have speedily fomented; the hands of royalty weighed too heavily upon their subjects to have justified even the thought of such an attempt. It was absolutely necessary that the starting point of such a venture should be far from those influences whose interests would incite them to crush it. When the time was ripe, Columbus discovered America, and thither for three hundred years the victims of civil and religious persecution fled for refuge, carrying with them sentiments of sincere affection for that civil and religious liberty that had been denied to them by their fatherland. In the comparative security of their new home they became independent in thought and action; their struggle for existence gave them bravery and fortitude, but it was only when they were numerous enough and rich enough to maintain themselves that the government of Great Britain inaugurated a system of tyrannical procedure that wise statesmanship could not avoid seeing would produce revolt.

The colonists were as devotedly loyal to King George as were their English kinsmen, until he scourged them into rebellion; the war for independence was not fought to found a Republic; the federal Union was an afterthought inspired by conditions. The Union was based upon certain vital principles of which the most important was that all men are created equal; yet the Union never would have been organized had not its constitution given the lie to its principles by at least impliedly recognizing human slavery. Seventy years afterwards there was civil war, brought about by slavery, yet that was not fought by the North to abolish slavery, but to maintain the Union. In the great uprising of the North that followed the assault upon Sumpter, the only thought was that our flag had been insulted and must be vindicated; that federal authority had been defied and must be restored; that the Union was in danger and must be saved. Hardly a man of all those who answered the call of Father Abraham anticipated the momentous result, and it is safe to say, that had that result been anticipated, had the abolition of slavery been the avowed object of the war, the attachment of our people to the constitution and to the rights of the states under it, was such that its successful prosecution would have been rendered doubtful, if not impossible.

It was only after McDowell had been routed at Bull Run, after McClellan had been driven from the peninsula, after Pope had been cut to pieces at Manassas, after Lee had carried the war into the north, and was flaunting the flag of secession at our very doors, that President Lincoln found sentiment ripe for the emancipation of the slaves. Then the abolition of slavery became a military necessity. But if conditions had been reversed, if the North had been victorious at Bull Run and McClellan had captured Richmond, who can doubt that the South would have preferred terms of peace or that the public opinion of the North would have gladly accepted the terms and would have restored the wayward sisters to all their old time rights including the maintainance of slavery? We cannot deny the truth; the great act of philantbropy that immortalized

Abraham Lincoln and shed enduring lustre upon the American Republic, was extorted by necessity, from hesitating, if not unwilling, hands. It was an overruling d vinity that shaped our ends. The events that led up to our present war with Spain, are no less notable.

We saw poor Cuba crushed under the iron heel of Spanish despotism. but we said "we must not interfere, it is not our country nor our business;" we saw its people, driven to despair, rise in revolution, yet we said, "we must not aid them, it is not our affairs;" we saw its patriot armies, half naked, poorly fed, fight against odds greater than our fathers fought against in our war for independence; we applauded their heroism, but we said "we can only give you our moral support;" we saw old men, women and children driven from their homes and left to starve; we heard their cries of despair, we heard their pleas for help; we saw them die, not by thousands but by hundreds of thousands, but we said, "we cannot interfere for intervention means war, and war costs men and money; besides we believe in the "splendid isolation" of the United States, but we assure you of our sympathy." We realized that the most corrupt, the most cruel, the most bigoted and most perfidious nation in the world, a robber and a butcher among nations, a nation whose long career fails to show a single act of magnanimous liberality, the intolerant foe of progress, the steadfast ally of despotism, whose crest should be a thumb screw and whose coat of arms should be a rack, we realized that this nation was waging war of extermination at our very doors against a people whose only crime was a determination to be free, but we refused to act until we were forced to act through the destruction of the Maine. Then we did what humanity had been bidding us to do for years, but what expediency and self-interest had prevented us from doing.

Truly, "there is a divinity that shapes our ends, rough hew them how we will."

THE LOSS AND GAIN OF WAR.

Having drawn the sword let us, as a united people, press forward, with undaunted fortitude, to that victory to which the justice of our cause entitles us. Our losses will be severe, but the glorious result is certain, and there are some gains that even ordinary intelligence can forecast that will far out weigh our loss.

OCCASIONAL WAR IS A NECESSITY TO THE WELFARE OF THE REPUBLIC.

To this country have come people of every nativity in constantly increasing floods of immigration. The best brai- and the strongest muscle of every civilized people is represented here, and one of the problems that presses upon consideration, is how to amalgamate these diverse elements, how to weld them into a common mass, united in customs, in institutions and in laws. The tree, transplanted, must take root among its new surroundings or it will die. The immigrant, whom our generous laws vest with almost instant citizenship, must, in justificatiou of that citizenship, become inspired with the same patriotic instincts towards his adopted country that it is natural for him to feel towards his fatherland. He must become endowed with the sense of proprietorship ; he must feel that this country is his country, that our flag is his flag ; his not by gift, not out of charity, but by right of service for it. He may admire the heroism of our revolutionary ancestors, but he cannot feel that pride in their achievements that he would feel if his ancestors had starved at Valley Forge or bled at Bunker Hill.

War is a creator of such patriotic feelings, the best educator to love for our flag and all that it symbolizes, because it creates traditions in which all who were concerned in it, must take a personal interest. I care not where he may have been born, no man passed through the fiery ordeal of the war for the Union without coming out an American citizen in the fullest sense of the term, and no man from Germany or Scandinavia, Great Britain or Ireland will fight for our flag in this war against Spain without being baptized into a love for his adopted country that he could gain in no other way.

ONE COUNTRY AND ONE FLAG.

But the greatest gain arises from the fact that the war will forever abolish sectional prejudice. Over shadowing all else, the harmony between the sections that is being promoted by this war, will be of priceless value. The "bloody chasm" that once divided the north from the south is filled with olive branches, and northern and southerner, as comrades now, march over it to the drum beat of the Union. Dewey of Vermont and Hobson of, Alabama vie with each other in heroic deeds. The last vestage of sectional bitterness lies buried with the Maine beneath the waters of the gulf, and Fitz Hugh Lee of Virginia at the head of Wisconsin men presses forward to revenge the wrong. At last, the Union is restored in sentiment as well as in form ; at last, we are one people acknowledging but one country and one flag ; at last we are prepared as a nation to go forward upon a glorious mission for which Divine Providence is marking out the way. That mission is not one of conquest ; as a Republic, our territory is already dangerously large, as a people, we should learn to govern ourselves before we undertake to govern others. But while avoiding territorial aggrandizement and equally avoiding international entaglements that would make us the tool of European ambition, we must submit to such modification of the theory of "splended isolation" as will enable the United States to exercise that influence for good that it is her province to exert.

Neither an individual nor a nation is created to live alone for selfish purposes; nations as well as individuals must contribute to the well being of their associates. For more than one hundred years the United States has tried to ignore this principle, moved by self interest; but when that principle was first promulgated we were the weakest, as we are now the strongest, we were the poorest, as we are now the richest nation in the world. If, under these changed conditions, America should now, without formal alliance, come to a understanding with that friendly nation whose hand has restrained the dogs of war from flying at our throat in aid of Spain, a new and glorious era for humanity will dawn; an era of civilization without war, of religion without persecution, of perfect liberty under the law.

When Mr. Elliott had concluded, Mr. Losey called for three cheers for the President of the United States, for the Army and Navy, and for the County and City of La Crosse, which were all given with a will. Before being dismissed the entire audience, led by the associated chorus and accompanied by the band, joined in singing

"AMERICA"

and with each succeeding stanza the harmonies swelled higher and higher, evincing an earnestness and depth of feeling almost

painful in its intensity. The meeting was then dismissed with a
benediction by the

Rev. S. L. McKee.

It was a scene never to be forgotten by those who participated.

THE CLOSING SCENES.

During the rest of the day the streets of the City presented an animated scene; the sidewalks of Main and the adjacent streets were utterly insufficient for the crowd of happy, smiling faces, and many had to take the "middle of the road."

After dark, when the artistic Memorial Arch had been lit up by thousands of electric lights, Main street became impassable, and continued so until the approaching fireworks drew off a portion of the crowd, permitting traffic to be resumed.

I do not feel equal to the task of describing the proceedings of the evening; they were entirely in the hands of the Committee on Regatta and the Committee on Fireworks, and as their reports tell the story better than I could, I herewith submit them.

COMMITTEE ON REGATTA.

On being appointed as a sole committee on Regatta, I at once called myself to order and proceeded to look over the ground, or rather the water. The committee found that La Crosse possesses a large fleet of steam, electric and naphtha launches, and was unanimous in the belief that a grand naval demonstration could and should be made. We at once put every vessel in commission and appointed the chairman admiral of the fleet. The fleet was ordered to assemble for preparatory manoeuvres and its cheerful response obviated the necessity of resorting to impressment. The Sea Dogs were apparently under the impression that they were required to assist in the bombardment of Manila, which formed so conspicuous a part of the programme of fireworks, and like the boys at Arcadia Fair, were bound to have three shots for a nickel at anything.

After a week of arduous drill during which the crews learnt the difference between fore and aft, could distinguish between starboard and port, could splice the main brace and learnt the locations

46

of the wine and shot lockers, it was found that they knew as much, and perhaps more, than the admiral.

On the evening of July 4th, about three bells, the fleet assembled under the protection of the central fort of the bridge leading to the Neutral Zone, and waited in anxious silence for the darkening shadows of departing day to enable them to steal upon the enemy and take him by surprise.

The fleet consisted of the South La Crosse, North La Crosse and Black River Squadrons and comprised the following vessels:
The Neche, battle ship, flying the pennant of the Admiral.
" Sunbeam, battle ship................Captain W. F. Funk,
" Nancy Roann, battle ship............Captain W. S. Cargill,
" Mabel, armoured cruiser.............Captain S. Y. Hyde,
" Iola, armoured cruiser..... ....Captain L. F. Easton,
" McKinley, armoured cruiser.........Captain Ben Ott.
" Sarah, armoured cruiser.............Captain J. C. Easton,
" Nellie, converted liner.......... ....Captain J. M. Hixon,
" Utopia, converted liner..............Captain John Willing,
" Edna, torpedo destroyer.............Captain C. Schroeder,
" Jenks, torpedo destroyer..... ....Captain John Jenks,
" Dora Nell, torpedo destroyer..........Captain C. H. Nichols,
" Otto, gunboat.....................Captain Otto Goetzky,
" No. 44, gunboat...................Captain Vic. Buschmann,
" Kitty, gunboat.........................Captain C. Oakins,
" Edna C., gunboat..................Captain W. W. Cargill,
" Great Eastern, dispatch boat...........Captain Wm. Tippets.

As the appointed hour drew near the Admiral ordered a reconnoisance in force, with a view to overawe the spectators and hurry up the firework operators. At four bells the fleet accordingly moved N. by N. E. in sailing order, doubled and formed in line of battle, and in formation of every known and unknown character, with the crews at general quarters, delivering a heavy fire of shells. rockets and bombs. There with the lights from the cabin windows and signal lanterns produced a pleasing and novel effect, at least the Admiral was so informed, but he cannot affirm it of his own knowledge, having been busy between decks overhauling the lockers, and as some of the fellows who so informed him are candidates for office, he gives their statement for what it is worth.

The crews by this time were getting impatient for the signal to attack Manilla, and were quivering with excitement, when a grape vine telegraph was received informing them that it was all over.

The Admiral at once gave the signal "Cease firing and go home," on which the fleet dispersed, highly pleased with the Admiral and themselves.

Respectfully submitted,

F. A. COPELAND,

Sole committee and (very) Rear Admiral.

COMMITTEE ON FIREWORKS.

The Committee on Fireworks on being appointed at once opened a correspondence with the leading firework makers of the Country, and after due deliberation selected a programme for which the cost was a secondary consideration, being determined to present a pyrotechnic display far excelling anything before seen in this city. It is difficult to foresee in advance and provide against the many little incidents, such as weather, etc., which help to make or mar the effect of a particular detail, but the committee feel free to claim that in all but one feature of the programme, the display was a great surprise to the many thousands who witnessed it. Notwithstanding the determination of the committee that their first object should be an exhibition worthy of the occasion regardless of cost, they kept within $250 of the amount appropriated to their use, and while—

" 'Tis not in mortals to command success,

They did far more, they studied to deserve it."

Respectfully submitted.

E. T. MUELLER,

Chairman.

The foregoing reports are interesting in themselves, and in addition possesses a certain degree of historical value; they record not only the proceedings of the day but also the systematic preparation made for their production. The enthusiastic liberality of the entire community made them possible, and the zeal and earnestness which animated all to whom the work was entrusted made them facts.

As will be seen by the report of the finance committee, the
amount received from all sources was.............. $3,465.30
The total expense................................ 2,724.06

Leaving a surplus of............................ $ 741.24
and the executive committee decided to return to the generous
subscribers twenty-five per cent. of the amount of their respective
subscription.

Each committee has made a detailed statement of the work
accomplished and presented vouchers for all expenditures. All
of them performed the work assigned to them with zeal and
energy and feel amply rewarded by the splendid success which
they jointly achieved.

The Chief Marshal, Colonel N. R. Nelson, performed his
laborious duties of organizing and arranging the grand, magnificent, industrial, historical and floral parade, over two miles in
length, for which he has received universal credit. His report
gives full details.

The President of the Day, J. W. Losey, conducted the
afternoon ceremonies with his proverbial ability, in a manner
worthy of the occasion.

The industrious and able Secretary, R. Calvert, has been the
soul of all committees; he deserves special recognition for his
unceasing and faithful performance of his duties. His introduc-
tory gives the full history of the preparatory work for the
celebration.

Through the efforts of E. B. Usher, Chairman, of the Historical Committee, a historical society was organized, which, no
doubt, will be of great and lasting value.

The city newspapers, the dailies: Chronicle, Republican
and Leader, Press and Abend Stern, also the weeklies, the
Argus, Nord Stern and Volksfreund, are all entitled to great
credit for their unanimous support and stimulations.

From the report of the committee on transportation, we had on that day over 8000 visitors from Iowa, Minnesota and parts of our own State; over twenty-five thousand people lined our beautifully decorated streets to witness the grand parade, as many were massed upon the river front to witness the magnificent display of fireworks and notwithstanding the immense crowds, not a theft was committed, not a pocket picked, not a breach of the peace took place, and not the slightest disorder or disturbance occurred.

Invitations to participate were extended to former citizens now residing at a distance, and many responded with congratulations and good wishes. Among these was ex-Mayor Joseph Clarke, who sent the following letter:

Philadelphia, Pa., June 27th, 1898.
MR. JOHN PAMPERIN, Chairman,
La Crosse, Wis.

MY DEAR SIR:

I thank you for your kind invitation of the 22nd, and I know of nothing that would give me greater pleasure than to take part in the celebration of Wisconsin's Semi-Centennial at La Crosse on the 4th of July. Until a few days ago, I looked forward to being in La Crosse at that time, but now find it will be impossible, and I sincerely regret it. But though absent in body, I will be with you in spirit. Every pulsation of my heart beats true to La Crosse and the legion of dear friends there.

I trust the celebration may be a great success and that prosperity may always attend the dear city.

With regards to all the ex-Mayors and all my friends, and to yourself personally, I am

Very truly yours,
JOSEPH CLARKE.

The present position of La Crosse in the scale of cities is presented at the close of this pamphlet and shows a wonderful growth in fifty years. Who can predict its future and that of our rich agricultural County. When the fifty years have ripened into a century, the prophetic eye sees a county with every acre teeming with the products of the soil for which the City will furnish a home market.

May not La Crosse then be a city of a hundred thousand people, its streets paved with brick and asphalt; it will assuredly have a water supply commensurate with its utmost needs, possibly fed from a reservoir on the top of Old Grandfather's Bluff, surrounded by a beautiful park, and many other advantages which are still in the womb of social and economic science, but it will not have a more patriotic, orderly and industrious people.

The executive committee at its final meeting also decided that the proceedings should be published in its present form for future reference, and as a permanent record of this great event in the history of the County of La Crosse. At that meeting the thanks of the body were extended to the newspapers of the city, the Chief of Police and Force, the Board of Public Works, and all the sub-committees who so faithfully aided in the work. Especial mention was made of the Chairmain and Secretary Calvert, but both of these officials disclaim any special merit, and on their behalf I embrace the opportunity of cordially endorsing the sentiments of the executive committee towards all concerned whose zealous cooperation made our labors a continual feast.

For myself, I feel amply rewarded in being privileged to say "I too am a Citizen of La Crosse."

Respectfully submitted,

JOHN PAMPERIN,
Chairman Exeutive Committee.

THE CITY OF LA CROSSE,

in the County of La Crosse, is the Second City in the State of Wisconsin, with a Population of 35,000.

AND IS THE GATEWAY TO AND FROM ALL OF THE GREAT WEST lying north of the 42d parallel of latitude; the entire trade between the east and that immense territory, both of domestic and imported staples going west and the cereals going seaward, must pass through it.

IS SITUATED at the confluence of the La Crosse and Black rivers with the Mississippi; the Black river being one of the largest pine timber rivers in the country, the product of which is all handled in La Crosse, furnishing employment to eleven large mills, with a capacity of over one million feet per day. It is also the outlet of all the pine and hardwood timber of the Wisconsin Valley seeking markets by rail.

HAS thriving manufactories of Boots and Shoes, Sash, Doors and Blinds, Plows, Agricultural Implements, Boilers and Heavy Machinery, extensive Carriage Works, Cracker and Knitting Factories, etc., large Flour Mills, Woolen Mills, a large Tannery, Mammoth Rubber Works, several Cooperages, five large Breweries, affording a market for 150,000 bushels of barley and 100,000 pounds of hops per annum; extensive cigar manufactories and various other industries.

HAS twenty-five miles of macadamized streets, thirty miles of water main and ten miles of street railway, operated by electricity.

HAS an efficient full paid Fire Department, and the best system of Water Works in the Northwest.

HAS four daily and six weekly newspapers and two religious monthlies, with an aggregate circulation of 26,260.

TWO Telephone Companies supply a first-class local service, and give long distance connections 1200 miles west of the Mississippi.

HAS fifty-five Churches, MODEL COMMON SCHOOLS, and a first-class HIGH SCHOOL and course.

HAS SIX PUBLIC HALLS, and its FOUR NEW OPERA HOUSES are acknowledged to be the most convenient and tastefully embellished in the Northwest.

HAS A FREE PUBLIC LIBRARY, with over 20,000 volumes, placed in a handsome building, erected in terms of a bequest of the late Hon. C. C. Washburn.

IS close to the hard timber forests and immense pineries; rates on coal and ore are always low, and for steam power its sawmills furnish fuel at an almost nominal cost.

HAS in its vicinity an inexhaustible supply of iron ore waiting development.

HAS the Mississippi river and eight railroads reaching in every direction, giving unsurpassed facilities for transportation.

HAS for a market the whole of Western Wisconsin, Northern Iowa, Middle and Southern Minnesota, and the twin states of North and South Dakota, a field which is practically unlimited.

HAS a large and increasing Jobbing Trade with these and other sections of the country, and the country storekeeper can have his wants as fully and cheaply supplied as in the eastern markets.

IS essentially the HOME OF THE WORKING MAN, with exceptional facilities for procuring CHEAP HOMES; as a result the laboring classes are mostly all freeholders, and a steady supply of labor can always be relied upon.

THE CITY is lighted by the Brush System of Electric Lighting and the Edison Incandescent System is largely used for interiors, both public and private. Coal gas is also supplied, both for light and fuel, at a reasonable rate.

ITS citizens are enterprising and extend a HEARTY WELCOME TO ALL NEWCOMERS, and the Board of Trade will cheerfully assist any one in looking for a desirable site, either in business or residence.

ADDRESS,

R. CALVERT, Secretary Board of Trade.

OFFICIALS, LA CROSSE COUNTY, 1898.

Chairman County Board............ ....W. C. Winter
Judge of County Court......................John Brindley
Sheriff......................................Gideon G. Lang
Deputy Sheriff........................... ......J. C. Follmer
Clerk Circuit Court......................... ....S. W. Brown
Register of Deeds.....................Randolph Elliott
District Attorney.................... ...John E. McConnell
County Clerk..... ....Milo J. Pitkin
County Treasurer..........................John Schild
County Surveyor.................. ...George P. Bradish
Superintendent of Schools................. ......C. E. Lamb

COUNTY BOARD.

Towns and Wards.	Supervisors.
Barre	George D. Sprain
Bangor	William Smith
Burns	John N. Jones
Campbell	C. H. Hawkins
Farmington	Frank Storandt
Greenfield	Herman Roesler
Holland	A. H. Bratberg
Hamilton	Frank P. Coburn
Onalaska	Valentine S. Keppel
Shelby	George A. Hosmer
Washington	Wenzel Korn
Village of West Salem	Jay Pettingill
City of Onalaska—	
First Ward	Edward Larson
Second Ward	Frank Pooler
Third Ward	Charles G. Hall
City of La Crosse—	
First Ward	Joseph Poehling
Second Ward	James A. Trane
Third Ward	Albert H. Akre
Fourth Ward	Frank M. Clark
Fifth Ward	Joseph Gale
Sixth Ward	Thomas Stavrum
Seventh Ward	Nels. R. Nelson
Eighth Ward	Edward C. Riley
Ninth Ward	John Streeter
Tenth Ward	John J. Durland
Eleventh Ward	William J. Gautsch
Twelfth Ward	Charles Spettle
Thirteenth Ward	Vincent Tausche
Fourteenth Ward	Charles S. Van Auken
Fifteenth Ward	George W. Young
Sixteenth Ward	Walter C. Winter
Seventeenth Ward	George Will, Jr.
Eighteenth Ward	Clemens Schaller
Nineteenth Ward	Solomon Burdick
Twentieth Ward	Andrew C. Kahler

OFFICIALS, CITY OF LA CROSSE, 1898.

Mayor...............................James McCord

City Clerk.............................J. M. Vrchota

City Treasurer............................M. Wannebo

City Comptroller.........................Fred Ring

City Attorney............................Martin Bergh

City Engineer.... ....Frank C. Powell

Police Justice. ....Leonard Kleeber

Chief of Police..........................H. H. Byrne

Chief of Fire Department....................C. A. Hunt

Board of Public Works } Silas F. Nice, David E. Bice, Carl Hanson

Tax Commissioner.....................Oswald Reichelt

Assessors....... ....A. H. Mitchell, Ole L. Myhre

Superintendent of Poor........ ....C. F. Scharpf

COMMON COUNCIL.

First Ward.............................Leo W. Meyer

Second Ward... ....A. P. Clark

Third Ward.............................Walter W. Scott

Fourth Ward............................Alfred James

Fifth Ward.............................Robert Schultze

Sixth Ward............................Thomas H. Spence

Seventh Ward..........................Henry E. Horne

Eighth Ward...........................John Falk

Ninth Ward........................ ... ..John Bergoust

Tenth Ward...........................Peter Nelson

Eleventh Ward. ....Frank W. Bartl

Twelfth Ward.........................Carl Ahrens

Thirteenth Ward......................John Koller

Fourteenth Ward......................S. B. Oatman

Fifteenth Ward... ....Paul Will

Sixteenth Ward.......................H. K. Vincent

Seventeenth Ward....................John Freehoff

Eighteenth Ward.....................James Sokolik

Nineteenth Ward.....................Peter Johnson

Twentieth Ward......................Frank Brown

56

MAYORS OF LA CROSSE, 1856 TO 1898.

Elected.

1856	Thomas B. Stoddard
1857	E. D. Campbell
1858	David Taylor
1859	James I. Lyndes
1860	John M. Levy
1861	Wilson Colwell
1862	A. W. Pettibone
1863 (re-elected)	A. W. Pettibone
1864 (re-elected)	A. W. Pettibone
1865	W. J. Lloyd
1866	John M. Levy
1867 (re elected)	John M. Levy
1868	Theodore Rodolf
1869	Charles L. Colman
1870	Theodore Rodolf
1871	Alex. McMillan
1872	James I. Lyndes
1873	G. Van Steenwyk
1874	G. M. Woodward
1875	James Hogan
1876 (re-elected)	James Hogan
1877	George Edwards
1778	David Law
1879 (re-elected)	David Law
1880	Joseph Clark
1881	H. F. Smiley
1882	David Law
1883 (re-elected)	David Law
1884	W. A. Roosevelt
1885	D. F. Powell
1886 (re-elected)	D. F. Powell
1887 (for two years)	David Austin
1889 (for two years)	John Dengler
1891 (for two years)	F. A. Copeland
1893 (for two years)	D. F. Powell
1895 (for two years)	D. F. Powell
1897 (for two years)	James McCord

www.ingramcontent.com/pod-product-compliance
Lightning Source LLC
Chambersburg PA
CBHW021640270326
41931CB00008B/1100